First Edition, 2025
Printed in the United States of America

moree-ny.com

ISBN 979-8-9936300-0-7

Library of Congress Control Number
2025923271

DOI: https://doi.org/10.17613/z1c8e-rvk19

ORCID: https://orcid.org/0009-0006-4978-600X

This booklet forms part of an ongoing research project examining the origins of Dada and the rediscovery of the painting Morée (c. 1915).

Further scholarly dialogue or curatorial inquiry is welcome.

moree.research@proton.me

Preface

Part I

Morée:

The First Half of *Étant donnés*

Part II

Preface

This study reconstructs the emergence of *Morée*, a painting made in New York about 1915–16 and later lost to history. Its surface—layered, eroded, and partially effaced—conceals a deliberate system of signs. Each mark carries intention: the vertical drips, the abraded signature, the theatrical ground, the suspended pearls.

From these fragments, a coded language emerges. The same logic reappears in Picabia's *Mistinguett* and finds resolution, decades later, in *Étant donnés*. Across this span, an idea persists: painting becomes experiment, expression concealment, authorship withdrawal.

Morée is singular in another way. It appears to authenticate itself, embedding within its own structure the logic and evidence of its origin. The painting functions as its own document—its own proof, independent and complete.

The pages that follow do not seek to solve the painting, but to reconstruct the conditions of its making—its place within the Arensberg circle, its kinship to the *Nudes*, and its echo in later works. What connects them is not style but intent: a strategy that turned painting into disappearance.

If *Morée* stands at the threshold of Duchamp's mature work, it marks the moment when meaning was buried by design, awaiting rediscovery through time itself.

This booklet records that return.

Morée

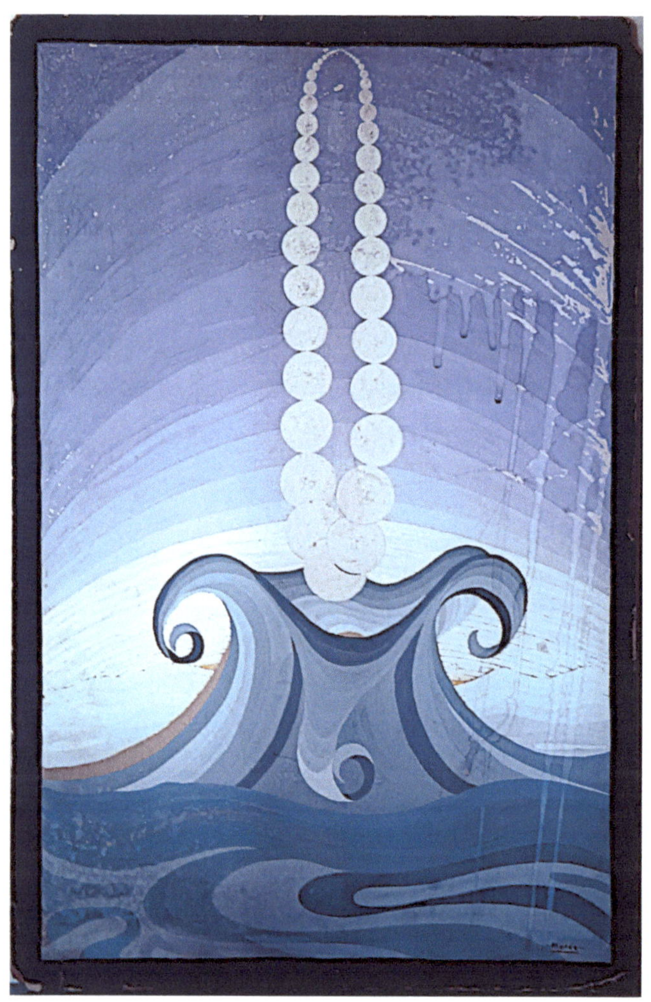

Morée

mor – from Latin mors, mortis: death.
ée, a feminizing suffix in French: "she who"

Together: *"she who has died"*.

Étant Donnés

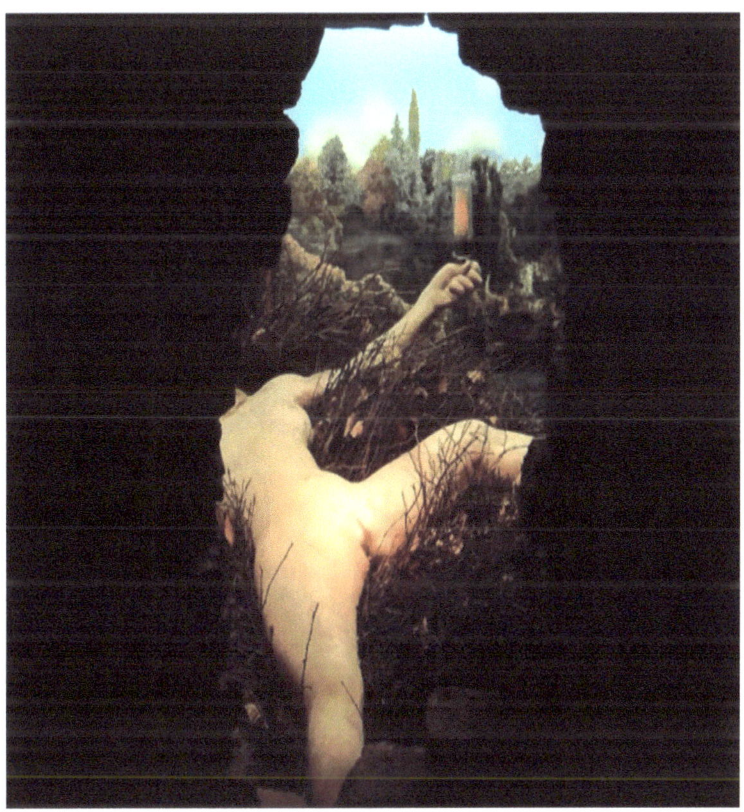

Full Title:
Étant donnés: 1° la chute d'eau, 2° le gaz d'éclairage…
(English: Given: 1. The Waterfall, 2. The Illuminating Gas…)

Both 1. *The Waterfall*, and 2. *The Illuminating Gas* are pointers that refer to *Morée*.

The *Waterfall* refers to the water stain in Morée. *The Illuminated Gas* is not the actual gas or even the lamp, but who it illuminates. It refers to ''she who has died'', the figural referent and named subject of *Morée*.

A Repeating Motif
— The Strand of Pearls —

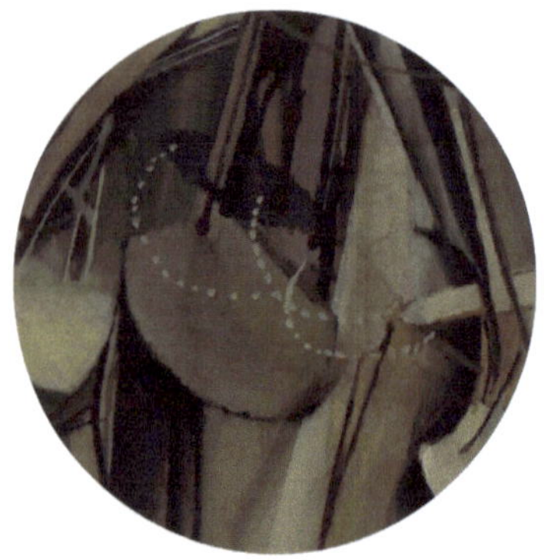

Nude No. 2 — 1912

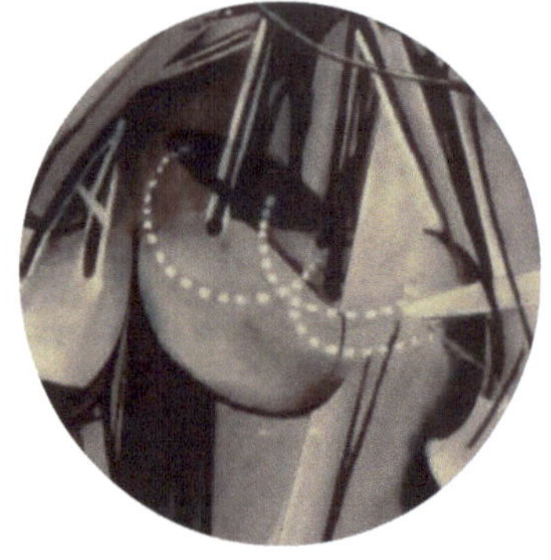

Nude No. 3 — 1916

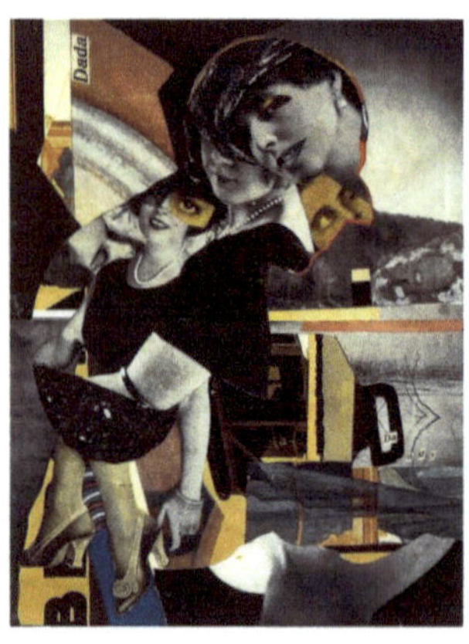

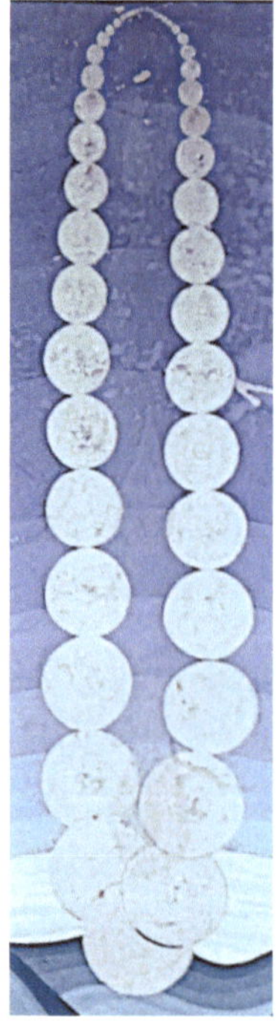

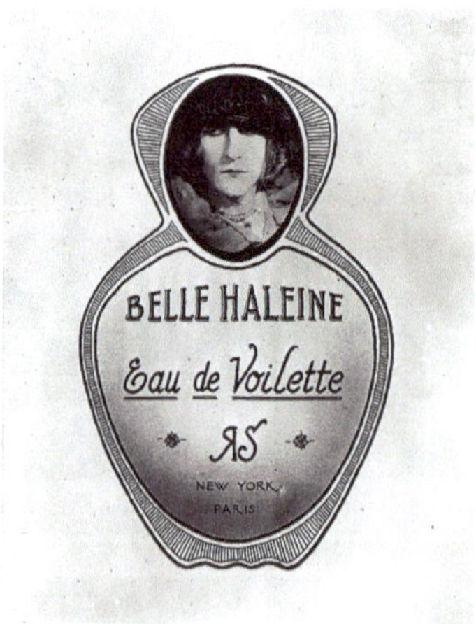

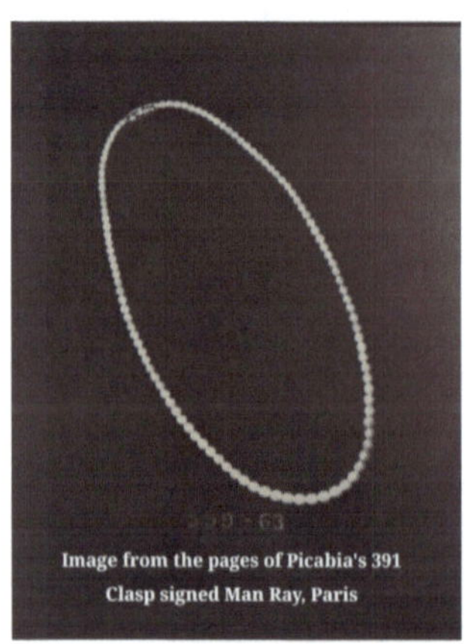

Image from the pages of Picabia's 391
Clasp signed Man Ray, Paris

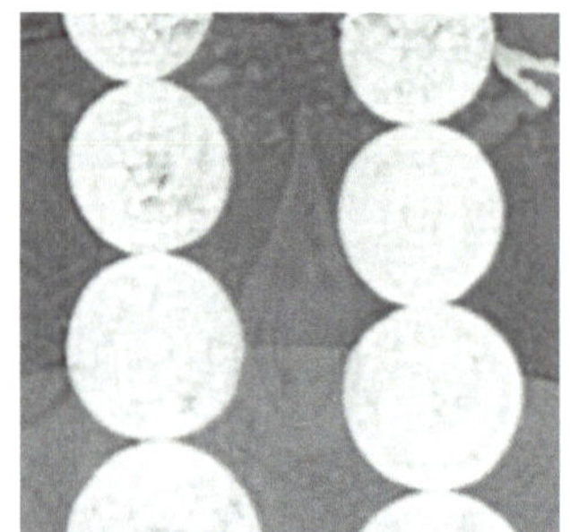

***Hidden Teardrops
Behind Pearls***

Part I
Morée: First Half of Étant donnés

This is not just the recovery of a lost painting, it is the exposure of a hidden system — a missing first half concealed in plain sight.

For half a century, *Étant donnés* (1969) has been treated as Marcel Duchamp's final gesture: a shocking tableau without precedent, an isolated climax to a career defined by rupture. Its unveiling was taken as the last word.

In July 1969, one year after Duchamp's death, the Philadelphia Museum of Art revealed the work to the public. Through two small holes in a heavy wooden door, visitors glimpsed a startling scene: a nude female figure sprawled in a rustic landscape, one arm raised to hold a glowing gas lamp, with a real waterfall cascading in the background. The effect was theatrical and unsettling — an orchestrated revelation glimpsed through the narrowest aperture.

At the time, this tableau was understood as an isolated shock. But it was never complete. *Étant donnés* was only the second half of a larger system, a concluding puzzle that secretly depends on another work created more than fifty years earlier. That painting — lost or misunderstood for decades — is *Morée* (1915/16).

Once recognized, *Morée* forces a radical revision. It reveals that Duchamp's farewell to painting was not abandonment but transformation: a coded burial that became the hidden first half of a cycle only completed with *Étant donnés*. The literal waterfall and lamp in the tableau were stage-prop distractions. The symbolic waterfall and buried pun of *Morée* unlock the entire structure.

The Camouflage

Duchamp's final work, *Étant donnés: 1° La chute d'eau, 2° Le gaz d'éclairage* (*Given: 1° The Waterfall, 2° The Illuminating Gas*), carried its solution on its face. For decades, the puzzle seemed closed. The real water in the tableau appeared to account for "1° The Waterfall." The glowing lamp seemed to fulfill "2° The Illuminating Gas." The title looked exhausted, the riddle solved.

But Duchamp was a master of misdirection. By giving each term a literal form, he built camouflage into the tableau — a theatrical solution designed to satisfy curiosity and prevent anyone from searching further. The waterfall and lamp were props, convincing enough to close the case but misleading enough to conceal the true origin.

The True Waterfall

That origin lies in *Morée*. Its background is slashed with vertical streaks where pigment has been deliberately lifted, simulating the look of water damage or theatrical erosion. At first they appear accidental, as if the painting had been neglected and left to decay. But these marks are staged.

They are the core of Duchamp's code: a symbolic "waterfall" disguised as entropy.

By constructing a literal waterfall in *Étant donnés*, Duchamp buried this earlier clue beneath a layer of realism. The staged waterfall of *Morée* was hidden by the real waterfall of the tableau. Only when the two are seen together does the disguise fall away.

The Illumination

The lamp does not represent "The Illuminating Gas." It is a decoy, a stage prop as deliberate as the waterfall. What matters is not the lamp itself, but what it illuminates: the nude body — lifeless, exposed, and pinned under its glare.

Here the title *Morée* becomes decisive. Split apart, it yields a double pun:

- *mor-* from Latin *mors, mortis*: death.

- *-ée*, a feminizing suffix in French: "she who."

Together: "she who has died."

The figure with the lamp reveals herself as *Morée* — naming herself not through literal illumination, but through illumination as revelation.

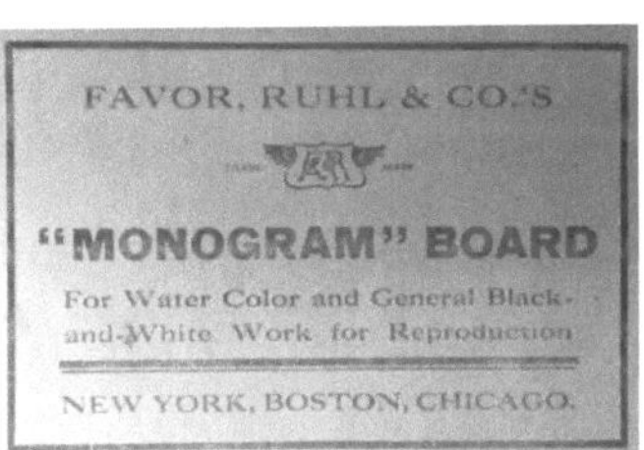

Early Morée Label
(from reverse)

The Structure Revealed

Both halves of Duchamp's title point back to the same painting:

- **1° The Waterfall → *Morée*.** The staged water stain is the true conceptual waterfall.

- **2° The Illuminating Gas → *Morée*.** Not the lamp itself, but the illuminating light that reveals "she who has died."

The real water and the glowing lamp inside *Étant donnés* were camouflage, persuasive but misleading props. Their function was to hold attention on the tableau and away from the hidden origin: the staged waterfall and fatal pun of *Morée*.

The Full Arc

With this recognition, Duchamp's career comes into focus. *Morée* is not a stray Dada experiment but the hidden first half of *Étant donnés* — staging the symbolic waterfall, encoding the pun of death, and marking the burial of painting. The tableau provides the second half, its literal waterfall and lamp masking their own source. Seen together, they reveal a cycle spanning five decades, and with it the truth: the supposed last word of Duchamp's career was never whole. The return of *Morée* rewrites his final work — and with it, the foundations of conceptual art.

The Private Meaning of Morée

If *Morée* completes the puzzle of *Étant donnés*, it also raises a deeper question: what did this painting mean to Duchamp at the moment of its creation? Why stage such a theatrical burial of meaning — and then conceal it for half a century?

Following the Clues

For Duchamp, the wound began a few years earlier. When *Nude Descending a Staircase, No. 2* was rejected from the 1912 Salon des Indépendants and later ridiculed in New York as a "machine gone mad," Duchamp was deeply affected.

Letters from that period, and later recollections by his brothers Jacques Villon and Raymond Duchamp-Villon's widow, confirm that he continued to "retouch" or "alter certain parts" of the painting after the Salon des Indépendants rejection. The original letters date to April-May 1912 several months before the paintings arrival in NY for the Armory show.

No photographs have surfaced showing the painting before the American Armory show, but their comments imply that the revisions were significant enough to warrant notice. The most likely candidates are the elliptical ring forms that appear near the torso of the descending figure — elements that seem stylistically distinct from the rest of the composition.

Within the broader trajectory of Duchamp's work, these three paintings — *Nude No. 2, Nude No. 3,* and *Morée* — when taken together, can be seen as an effort to clarify what had been misunderstood in *Nude No. 2* and to lay it finally to rest.

If the elliptical rings were added between the 1912 *Salon des Indépendants* and the 1913 *Armory Show,* they may represent an attempt by Duchamp to re-humanize a figure already dismissed as mechanical.

After *Morée*, misunderstanding itself became part of Duchamp's method: not something to correct, but something to orchestrate.

The Signature

The name "..Morée..." flanked by two dots before and three after, is not decoration. It encodes a lost sequence: two dots for *Nude No. 2* and three for *Nude No. 3.* Placing the name between them situates *Morée* in time — precisely between the two *Nudes,* marking the moment when the figure was orignally put to rest.

Linguistically, Morée names the Nude herself — "she who has died" — making her the very subject of mourning.

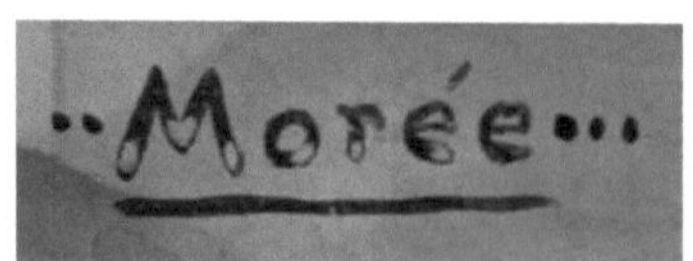

Moree Signature

Morée (1915/16): The True Farewell

A few years after painting Nude Descending a
Staircase No.2, Duchamp responded with *Morée*,
a painting that is at once theatrical, mournful, and
devastatingly final.

Pearls Tossed Into a Waiting Wave

In *Morée*, the misunderstood rings return as **literal
pearls**, now unmistakable.
But they do not rest serenely in place.
They are shown **mid-motion**, as though **hurled
forward**, their arc descending toward the curling form
of a **stylized wave** at the base of the composition.

This is the painting's central drama:
The very symbol critics failed to read in *No. 2* is now
offered up and cast away, sacrificed to a ritual act of
destruction.

The wave is not chaotic or naturalistic.
It is **theatrical and ceremonial**, like a stage prop —
the focal point of a deliberate performance.

The Hidden "Waterfall"

Behind this action lies a second, subtler device: a field
of **vertical streaks** that resemble **ordinary water
damage**, as though the painting had been left to decay
over time.

At first glance, they appear accidental — traces of age or neglect rather than deliberate design.

But this illusion is deliberate. These streaks are **carefully composed**, a staged form of erosion. They are the true "Waterfall" Duchamp later encoded in the title of *Étant donnés*.

Thus, the painting operates on two levels:

1. **Foreground:** A symbolic sacrifice — pearls being tossed into a theatrical wave.

2. **Background:** A perfect camouflage — the illusion of decay, pretending to be natural when it is in fact staged.

A Painting That Buries Itself

The heavy **black border** surrounding *Morée* makes its purpose unmistakable. Like the black frame used in printed obituaries or mourning notices, it signals death and memorialization.

What is being buried here is not just the feminine figure, but **painting itself**:

- The Nude, misunderstood and destroyed.

- The art form, abandoned by Duchamp as a medium for thought.

- The artist himself, whose scraped signature and pseudonymous *Morée* together enact his withdrawal — one through erasure, the other through disguise.

Seen in this light, *Morée* is not a continuation of Duchamp's painting career.

It is a **farewell performance**, a theatrical burial staged in plain sight.

Nude Descending a Staircase No. 3
October 1916

After completing *Morée*, Duchamp appears to have regarded his painterly investigations as finished. Its self-reflexive structure—coded authorship and the corrosive treatment of surface—had exhausted the medium's possibilities for him. Yet at the insistence of Walter Arensberg, his closest patron and ally, Duchamp revisited *Nude Descending a Staircase (No. 2)*, completing *Nude Descending a Staircase (No. 3)* in October 1916. Contemporary evidence suggests that this third version was less an act of inspiration than of obligation—a commissioned reiteration that confirmed his departure from painting rather than extending it.

Two subtle but decisive deviations set *No. 3* apart:

Clarified Rings → Pearls:

- In *No. 2*, the rings were too subtle and easily misread.

- In *No. 3*, Duchamp **clarifies their structure**, making them visually closer to the literal pearls of *Morée*.

This is not an attempt to salvage meaning but a private acknowledgment of what had been lost.

The Black Border:

Duchamp again incorporates a **black border** around the composition, this time a photographic border.

At the time, this seemed decorative and went unremarked.

Now, in light of *Morée*, it is revealed as a **mournful echo** — a photographic version of *Morée*'s memorial frame.

Through these changes, Duchamp makes clear — without a word — that Arensberg's Nude had already died.

Nude Descending a Staircase No. 2

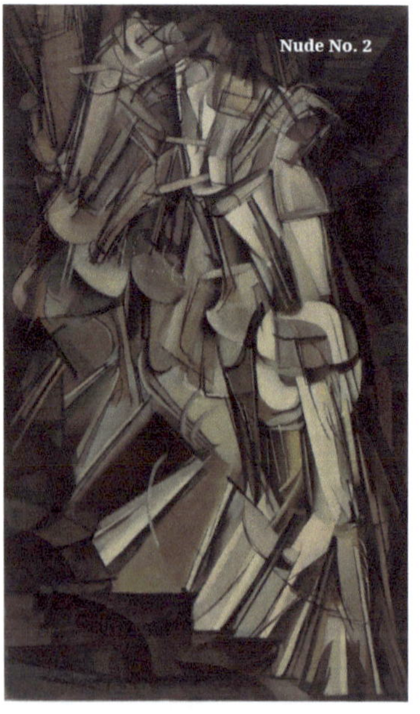

Marcel Duchamp — Philadelphia Museum of Art, Philadelphia, PA

Nude Descending a Staircase No. 3

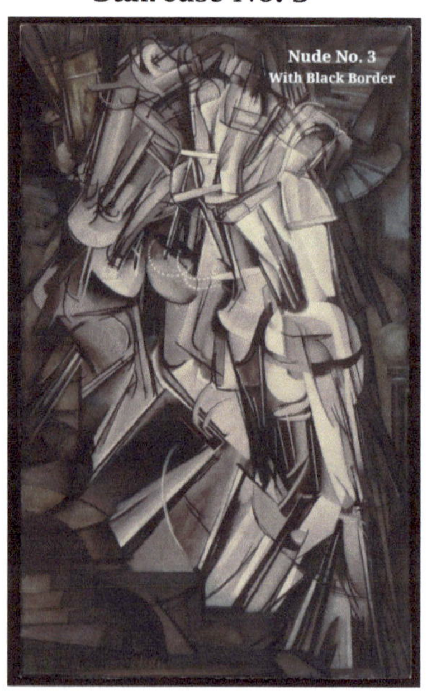

Marcel Duchamp — Philadelphia Museum of Art, Philadelphia, PA

Morée as Turning Point
The Full Sequence

Taken together, three works trace a precise arc. In 1912, *Nude Descending a Staircase, No. 2* introduced the motif of the pearl-like rings, but critics dismissed them as mechanical gears or motion lines.

What Duchamp had meant as a subtle feminine inflection — a rhythm of descent rather than a diagram of machinery — was lost in translation. The misunderstanding isolated him from both Cubism and Futurism and set in motion his gradual withdrawal from painting.

In *Morée* (1915–16), the motif returns in full awareness of that failure. The rings have become literal pearls, suspended within a dramatic, unstable field whose drips and abrasions suggest corrosion rather than motion.

The black border, far from decorative, reads as a sign of mourning — for painting, for the *Nude*, and for the possibility of direct meaning itself. Each mark feels deliberate yet self-erasing, as though the painter were testing how much could be removed before the image disappears. The result is not a portrait or abstraction but an act of negation, where depiction and disappearance coincide.

Then, by October 1916, *Nude Descending a Staircase, No. 3* repeated the motif once more. The rings were clarified, now unmistakably pearls, and the black border reappeared as a formal echo — a final gesture of acknowledgment rather than invention, reaffirming the mourning band first laid down in *Morée* for the *Nude No. 2* that had already died.

The work ends the sequence quietly, confirming what *Morée* had already decided: that painting could no longer sustain the kind of revelation Duchamp was after.

Morée is where he said goodbye — not only to painting, but to authorship as a form of control. The scraped signature and subdued tone are both confession and strategy: the point where authorship is withdrawn so that meaning can emerge elsewhere, in the act of recognition rather than creation.

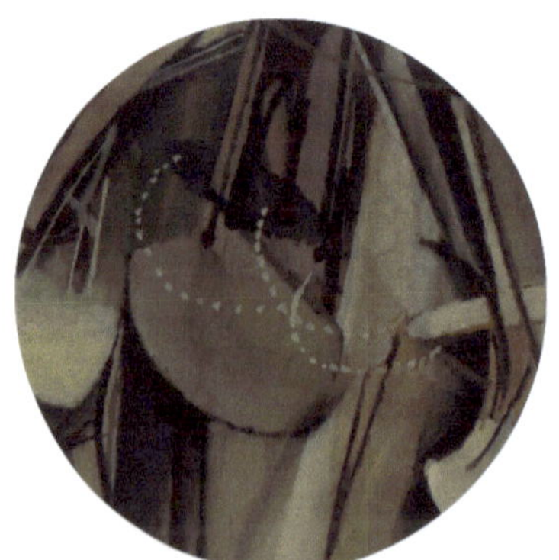

Nude No. 2 — 1912

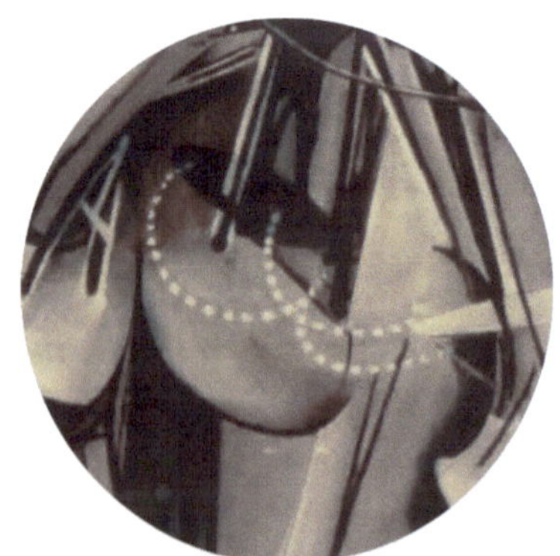

Nude No. 3 — 1916

The Roots of Étant donnés

The following note, drafted circa 1914–15 and later linked to Duchamp's Green Box material, outlines the conceptual structure that would govern Étant donnés.

Its language of "instantaneous rest" and "extra-rapid exposition" provides a key to understanding *Nude Descending a Staircase*—and to recognizing its later echo in *Morée*.

Note: The following text — referred to here as *The Préface* — was written circa 1914-1915, though it was not called that at the time.

The Préface

Étant donnés: 1° the waterfall / 2° the illuminating gas, we will determine / the conditions / of the Instantaneous Rest (or allegorical appearance) / of a succession [or set] of random facts / seeming to necessitate one another / according to laws, in order to isolate the sign / of the concordance between, on the one hand, / this Rest (capable of every eccentricity) / and, on the other hand, a selection of Possibilities / legitimated by these laws and also occasioned by them.

For instantaneous rest = to bring in / the extra-rapid expression.

We will determine the conditions for the best / exposition of the extra-rapid Rest [or extra-rapid pose] (= allegorical appearance) / of a set… etc. / nothing maybe.

Étant donnés (in darkness) 1° the waterfall,
or, given 2° the illuminating gas, in darkness, / we will
determine the conditions of the extra-rapid exposition
(= allegorical appearance) / of several collisions
seeming to succeed one another rigorously / each to
each according to laws, in order / to isolate the sign of
the concordance between this / extra-rapid exposition
(capable of every eccentricity) on the one hand / and
the choice of possibilities legitimated by these laws on
the other hand.

a a being the exposition / b b " the possibilities

the ratio a/b lies entirely not in a / number c (a/b = c)
but in the sign (a/b) which separates / a and b; as
soon as a and b are "known" they become / new units
and lose their relative numerical value (or of duration);
/ what remains is the sign (a/b) that separated them
(sign of the / concordance or rather of …? … search).

The Photographic Logic of "Instantaneous Rest"

When Duchamp writes of "extra-rapid exposition," he is using the vocabulary of photography.

In French, *exposition* meant "exposure" — the time light strikes a photographic plate. Around 1910–1915, manuals described high-speed cameras with the same phrase: *exposition ultra-rapide.* Duchamp's pairing of this term with "instantaneous rest" defines a central paradox of modern vision — motion represented only through its arrest.

The faster the exposure, the more completely movement disappears. "Instantaneous rest" is not the opposite of motion but its technological consequence.

Nude Descending a Staircase and the Language of Exposure

This is the logic behind *Nude Descending a Staircase No. 2* (1912).

Like the motion studies of Marey and Muybridge, the painting compresses a sequence of exposures into a single image. Each overlapping form functions as an "instantaneous rest" — a still moment within a continuous descent. The work translates photographic time-slicing into the pictorial field.

By 1912, Duchamp had turned the mechanical record of motion into a conceptual problem: how to represent time once photography had made motion visible. The *Nude* was his first answer.

Morée at the Threshold of Collision

Morée (1915–16) marks the point where Duchamp's exploration of motion-in-stillness reached its limit. The challenge was no longer how to depict motion, but how to **arrest the instant before impact**—when a rising wave lifts to meet the pearls flung toward it. What appears as calm aftermath is, on closer reading, a scene of suspended convergence: a poised collision in which ascent and fall merge into a single act of hesitation. The painting holds that equilibrium between approach and contact—**a choreography of forces under pressure**.

Morée occupies not the residue of motion but its most volatile threshold. The scene remains in tension, neither resolved nor released. It is the stillness of anticipation, not rest. The "waterfall" of *The Préface* finds its counterpart here—not as motion frozen, but as motion conscious of its own suspension.

The dotted pseudonym performs a parallel operation— what Duchamp later called the *"sign of concordance"*: a reconciliation between author and image, motion and rest, exposure and concealment.

In *Morée*, these opposites no longer contend but coexist under a fragile truce. Together, they declare not merely the end of an artistic phase, but the closure of painting itself.

From Motion to Apparition: The Continuation in Étant donnés

More than fifty years later, *Étant donnés* resumes the terms of *The Préface* — "the waterfall" and "the illuminating gas" — but translates them into a fixed tableau. The viewer now performs the act of exposure by looking through the peepholes, yet nothing moves. The scene exists in perpetual suspension, as if frozen by the camera's shutter.

Étant donnés is therefore not an innovation but a restatement: the *Nude*'s motion and *Morée*'s stasis recombined into a single, perpetual image.

Summary

The language of "instantaneous rest" and "extra-rapid exposition" emerges directly from photography. Duchamp first translated it into painting with *Nude Descending a Staircase*, then declared its exhaustion in *Morée*, and finally reanimated it mechanically in *Étant donnés*.

The three works trace a continuous argument about representation itself — how to picture what has already stopped moving.

** Instantané" and "exposition ultra-rapide" appear in Kodak and Lumière manuals ca. 1910–1915, confirming the photographic resonance of Duchamp's phrasing.*

The Waterfall Effect

The background of *Morée* is built around a vertical pattern of drips and suspended forms. The paint runs downward in narrow, uneven streams that stop abruptly before reaching the bottom edge. This is not an accident of handling. It is a deliberate structure — a controlled image of descent arrested in mid-flow.

The "waterfall" effect defines the logic of the painting. It turns gravity into composition, transforming liquid movement into fixed trace. The surface shows evidence of motion, but nothing moves. Each drip records an event that has already ended.

In *Morée*, this effect serves as both image and idea. It represents a fall that has already occurred — an act of release followed by restraint. The result is a surface that appears alive but remains still, a balance between action and its residue.

Technical Process

The effect was achieved not by adding paint, but by removing it. The darker surface layer appears to have been partially dissolved or stripped away, revealing a violet underlayer beneath. This subtractive process would explain the crisp edges and irregular transparency of the vertical drips — characteristics inconsistent with gravity-driven flow alone.

A water–alcohol mixture was probably used to create this clean, controlled erosion. Such a solution would have lowered the surface tension of the upper layer, allowing sections of the pigment to lift or slide away while leaving the underlying tone intact.

The resulting boundaries show evidence of the Marangoni effect — the physical phenomenon in which variations in surface tension cause liquid to pull away from areas of lower tension. This produces the tapered, feathered edges visible in the descending bands, a natural outcome of the differential drying between alcohol and water.

Morée

Privately Owned

The "waterfall" of *Morée*, then, is not a depiction but a material event — a staged chemical reaction captured in paint. What reads as descent is, in fact, exposure: the unveiling of the base layer through the controlled removal of the one above.

Implications for Later Works

Understanding this process clarifies several later echoes. In Picabia's *Mistinguett*, the physical scratches and fingerprinted drips can be read as literalized versions of *Morée*'s subtractive gesture — interventions that damage the surface to reveal meaning beneath. In Arensberg's poem *Theorem*, the visual language of veiling and exposure repeats the same logic in another form: the act of revelation achieved through description.

The Drip as a Calling Card

In New York Dada, one element recurs with uncanny persistence: the drip. Whether a streak, cascade, or blemish, it serves as a hidden signature — proof that a work belongs to a deeper network. The origin lies with Morée. Its staged waterfall, disguised as damage, introduced a radical idea: erosion could be performed — decay crafted as code. Duchamp's brilliance was to make these first "drips" seem accidental; viewers would have thought they were seeing entropy, not design. From then on, every Dada drip carried this charge — undermining surfaces, corrupting images, masking authorship as chance.

A compelling early echo appears in Francis Picabia's *Mistinguett* 1917. Where Duchamp hid sabotage under accident, Picabia made it overt. Drips run down the surface, slashed by fingerprints that expose destruction as performance.

A black pool recalls the dark wash that once veiled Morée: Duchamp had rinsed pigment to reveal violet beneath, and Picabia translates that act of removal into physical scratches through the pool — an echo of Duchamp's abraded signature.

Most striking is a zig-zagging red drip curling from the pool. The pigment recoils from it, mimicking the Marangoni effect — one liquid pulling from another. In Morée, Duchamp likely used alcohol and water to induce this, giving decay chemical precision; Picabia paints the process directly, turning the hidden act into visible code.

Mistinguett can be understood as an early echo of Morée's staged erosion, visible in the fingerprinted drips and surface disruptions. The two form a concealed pair: Morée as Duchamp's private act of sabotage, *Mistinguett* as Picabia's reply. Their dialogue, though unseen, marks the moment when mourning became a shared, clandestine language of sabotage.

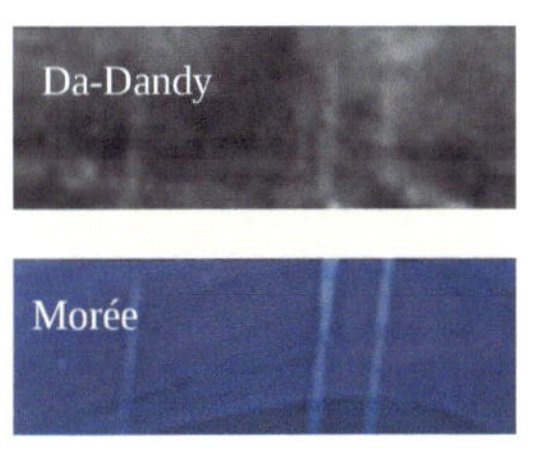

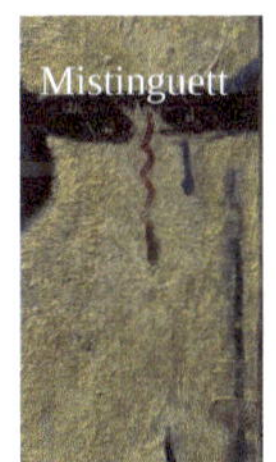

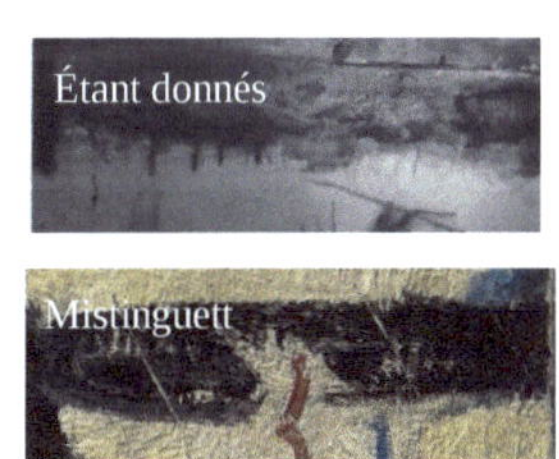

The Drip as a Calling Card

Theorem:
The Painting Put Into Words

In May 1917, the second and final issue of Duchamp's magazine *The Blind Man* carried a strange text credited to Walter Arensberg. Titled *Theorem*, it promised logic but delivered riddles: part poem, part puzzle, entirely unreadable to casual readers. For over a century it has been dismissed as another scrap of Dada nonsense. In fact, it is a veiled description of *Morée* — the only time Duchamp allowed the painting to surface publicly, not as image but as text.

The strategy behind *Theorem* mirrors the strategy of *Morée*:

- *Morée's* staged waterfall looked like accidental decay, concealing sabotage in plain sight.

- *Theorem's* cryptic lines looked like meaningless wordplay, concealing a precise description of that same painting. For those who had actually seen *Morée* — Duchamp, Arensberg, Picabia, and a small inner circle — the poem's imagery would have been legible. To everyone else, it was opaque. This duality let Duchamp seed evidence in public print while keeping the painting hidden.

Theorem

Theorem

For purposes of illusion
                    the actual ascent of two waves
                              transparent to a basis
                              which has a **disappearance** of its own
is timed
          at the angle of incidence
                              to the swing of a suspended
                                                lens
from which the waves wash
                         the protective coloration.
Through the resultant exposure
                         to a temporal process
an emotion
          ideally distant
                         assumes on the uneven surface
                                                descending
          as the identity to be demonstrated
the three dimensions
                    with which it is incommensurate.

WALTER CONRAD ARENSBERG.

Theorem with annotations

Theorem

For purposes of illusion
                    the actual ascent of two waves (The Rising Wave)
                              transparent to a basis (A Semi-transparent Top Layer
                              which has a disappearance of its own
                                                Dissolving or Washing Away)
is timed
          at the angle of incidence (Swinging Pendant Meets Rising Wave in Time and Space)
                              to the swing of a suspended (Suspended Lens is a Metaphor
                                                lens   for String of Pearls)
from which the waves wash
                         the protective coloration. (Revealing the Base Layer)
Through the resultant exposure
                         to a temporal process
an emotion
          ideally distant   (Describing the Formation of Drips)
                         assumes on the uneven surface
                                                descending
          as the identitiy to be demonstrated (Nude Descending a Staircase No. 2)
the three dimensions
                    with which it is incommensurate. (A Painting)
                    WALTER CONRAD ARENSBERG.

From Painting to Print

Placed in sequence, the timing is exact:

1. 1915–16: Duchamp creates *Morée* in private.

2. October 1916: finishes *Nude No. 3*, long unrecognized as a coded memorial.

3. April 1917: *Fountain* scandal erupts.

4. May 1917: *Theorem* publishes the painting in coded language.

5. Mid-1917: Picabia paints *Mistinguett*, translating the sabotage back into visual form.

Rather than reproducing the painting outright — which would have exposed too much — Duchamp displaced it into language, then let Picabia retranslate it into image. The code was moving laterally: painting → print → painting again.

Poetic Evidence

This text is not whimsy but intent. It proves Duchamp and Arensberg were systematically binding a private painting to public acts, using poetry as camouflage. Even if *Morée* were lost, *Theorem* preserved its trace. If it ever resurfaced, the poem would act as a key, confirming Duchamp had marked it at the height of Dada's eruption.

Francis Picabia's *Mistinguett*

Around mid-1917, Francis Picabia painted *Mistinguett*, a work that seems to share a private conversation with *Morée*. Both appear to have been conceived within the same brief interval when Duchamp and Picabia were exchanging ideas in New York. Yet their fates diverged: *Morée* remained in America; *Mistinguett* likely traveled back to Paris with Picabia, where it vanished from view for more than three decades. Finally resurfacing when Pierre Granville purchased it in 1952.

In 1966 the Guggenheim acquired the painting from Granville. Its later catalogue recorded the provenance with a single, telling remark: **"early history unknown."**

The phrase could hardly be more fitting. *Mistinguett* emerged from obscurity as if from deliberate concealment—an image waiting for its receiver. Its meaning would remain suspended for the next seventy years, only becoming legible once the reappearance of *Morée* exposed the two works as parts of the same, deliberately divided idea.

Twin Systems on Separate Shores

Each painting enacts a form of controlled erosion. In *Morée*, vertical drips stage the illusion of damage; in *Mistinguett*, the drips are painted outright, then crossed by fingerprints that literalize the act of sabotage. What Duchamp renders as hidden procedure, Picabia translates into a visible script. They are two halves of one system—composed apart but speaking the same coded language.

Surface and Trace

A dense black field anchors the right side of
Mistinguett, corresponding to the dark wash that once
veiled sections of *Morée.* Where Duchamp's layer was
rinsed away, Picabia scores and scratches his surface,
turning absence into mark. Both artists transform
destruction into structure, erasure into authorship. The
dialogue between them unfolds through acts of
negation: one washes away, the other incises, each
testing the limits of visibility and control.

The Vanishing Signal

Later in life, Picabia reportedly wondered what had
become of "that *Mistinguett* painting," as though
aware that its disappearance carried meaning of its
own. The long silence between creation and
rediscovery becomes part of the work's internal logic
—a literal delay that mirrors Duchamp's fascination
with art as postponed communication. The lost years
do not interrupt the story; they *complete* it.

One Idea, Two Destinies

Seen together, *Morée* and *Mistinguett* suggest a
transatlantic experiment in concealment and
revelation. Their shared motifs—drips, abrasions, and
theatrical darkness—encode the same gestures of
refusal, one remaining in New York, the other carried
into European exile. Whether by design or by chance,
the gap of thirty-five years and the official record's
quiet verdict—"early history unknown"—complete the
gesture: the work survives only through disappearance,
its signal transmitted not by exhibition but by delay.

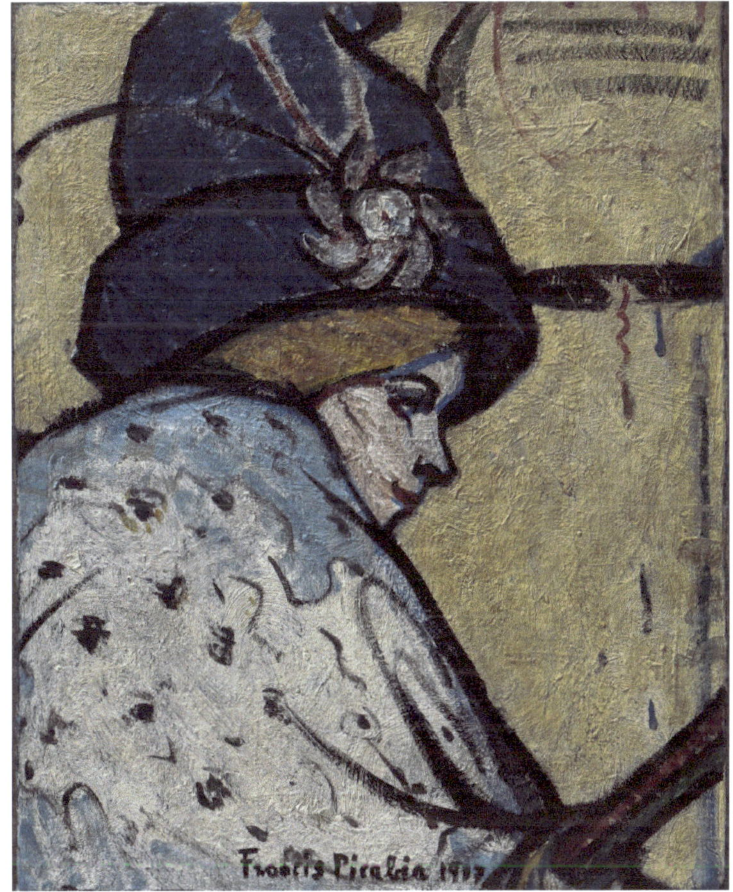

Francis Picabia — Solomon R. Guggenheim Museum, New York, NY

Da-Dandy and a Possible Rebuke

By 1919, Duchamp's private system of coded gestures — first seen in *Morée* and echoed in Picabia's *Mistinguett* — seems to have faced its first breach. This came from **Hannah Höch**, whose photomontage *Da-Dandy* combines three elements too precise to be coincidence:

1. **Pearls** – echoing Duchamp's motif from *Morée*, where they had shed their ornamental role and assumed a deeper symbolic meaning.

2. **A halftone background** – a printed image that merges two distinct sources:

   - The **drip motif of *Morée***, subtly embedded in its pattern.

   - A **collage by Joseph Stella**, another figure tied to Duchamp's NY circle.

This hybrid backdrop suggests that Höch not only saw the printed halftone but also absorbed its meaning, which likely leaked through the Dada network surrounding Duchamp's circle.

3. **A looming male silhouette** – strongly resembling Duchamp himself, implying that the title *Da-Dandy* may literally **name him**.

Viewed together, these elements form a **public provocation**.

Höch doesn't just parody bourgeois femininity; she appears to **cut up Duchamp's private code** and paste it into her own collage, pulling secret symbols into the open. If deliberate, this was a direct challenge to Duchamp and his tightly guarded system.

Duchamp's Retaliation: *Watch Your Step*

Duchamp answered — not through confrontation, but through **coded retaliation**.

In 1921 he issued a playful/cutting advertisement, carrying two pointed messages:

- **"WATCH YOUR STEP!"** – a sharp warning that Höch had stepped into dangerous territory she didn't understand.

- **"CUT OUT DADYNAMIC STUFF!"** – a double-edged pun:
    - **"Cut out"** refers both to collage cutting and to stopping altogether.
    - **"Dadynamic"** fuses *Dada* and *dynamic*, mocking the chaotic, theatrical energy of Berlin Dada and its Futurist-inspired visual motion.

Read together, it says: *Stop cutting and stop meddling with Duchamp's private system.*

Da-Dandy

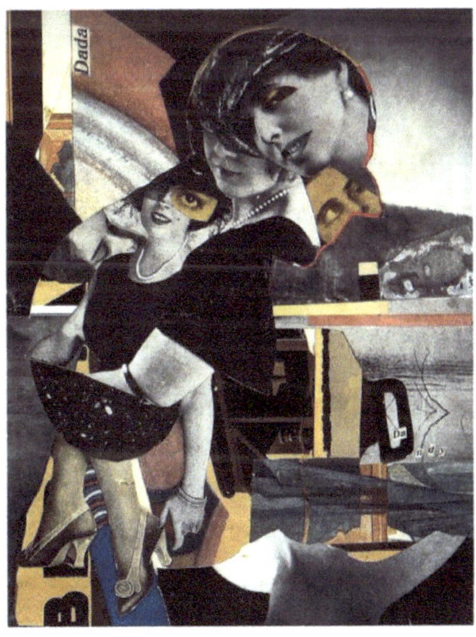

Hannah Höch — Privately Owned

The image of a high-heeled foot literalizes the warning: Höch has taken a step too far, and Duchamp is ready to trip her up.

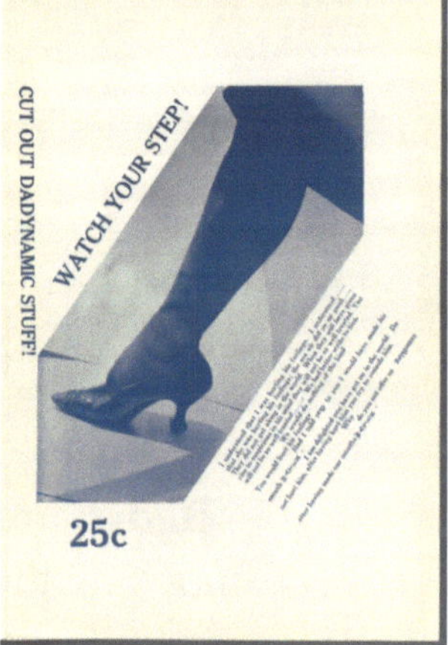

Aftermath: Pushing the Motif Underground

This public warning marked a turning point.
The staged drip motif, now compromised, would be **pushed underground**:

- It appears **one final time** in 1921's *Belle Haleine*, so faintly rendered it nearly disappears into the background.

- After that, it vanishes entirely, not resurfacing until Duchamp's hidden final work, *Étant donnés*, decades later.

Da-Dandy thus becomes a pivotal moment:
the first time Duchamp's private symbols were **used without permission**, and the moment he realized that concealment was no longer just strategy — it was survival.

Belle Haleine — 1921
A Final Whisper

In collaboration with Man Ray, Duchamp created
Belle Haleine: Eau de Voilette, a found perfume bottle
relabeled with a parody advertisement.
At first glance, it reads as a playful joke — Duchamp
posing as his female alter ego, **Rrose Sélavy**, on a
commercial label.

But hidden in the design are subtle **vertical streaks**,
barely perceptible. To casual viewers, they look like
simple background decoration. To those who know
Morée, they are unmistakable: the **waterfall motif**,
now reduced to the thinnest possible trace.

The title encodes this retreat:

- *Eau de Voilette* means **"Veil Water"**, directly
  naming the staged waterfall effect first seen in
  Morée.

- The label also functions as camouflage:
  Duchamp hides the drip motif in plain sight,
  within a photographic backdrop.

- The parody breathes the last trace of *Morée's*
  waterfall into vapor and wordplay.

This work marks Duchamp's strategic withdrawal:

- The staged drip is still present, but only insiders will notice it.

- It is Duchamp's way of reclaiming the motif after Höch's public intrusion, hiding it within his own circle.

Belle Haleine

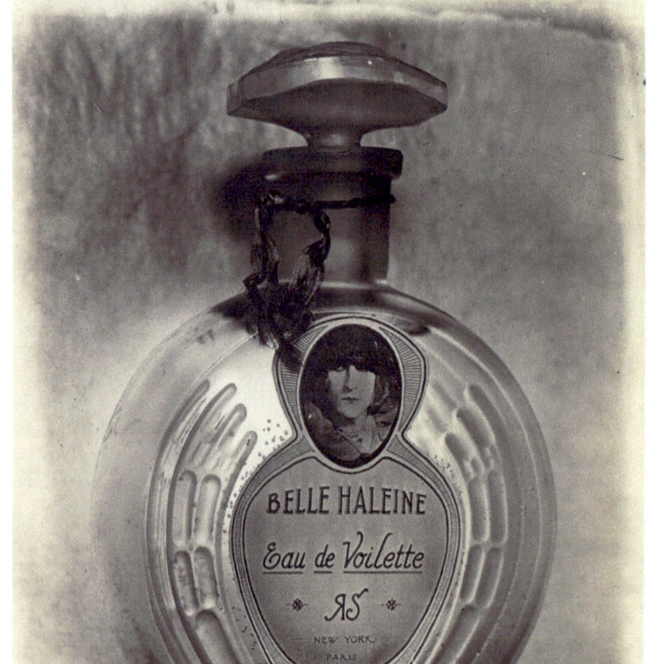

Marcel Duchamp, Man Ray — Museum of Modern Art, New York, NY

Echoes and Extensions:
Possible Parallels to *Morée's* Logic

Several later Dada works appear to revisit the same strategies first seen in *Morée*: obstruction, erasure, and the transformation of everyday materials into acts of refusal. Each of these examples—by Duchamp and Man Ray—seems to take one of *Morée's* underlying operations and develop it in a new medium.

Fresh Widow converts transparency into blockage; *The Gift* turns usefulness into contradiction; and *Pearl Necklace* returns to the motif of suspended pearls as a self-contained image. Together they suggest that *Morée's* language of interruption—its careful balance between revelation and concealment—persisted as a shared undercurrent in later Dada works.

Marcel Duchamp, Fresh Widow (1920)

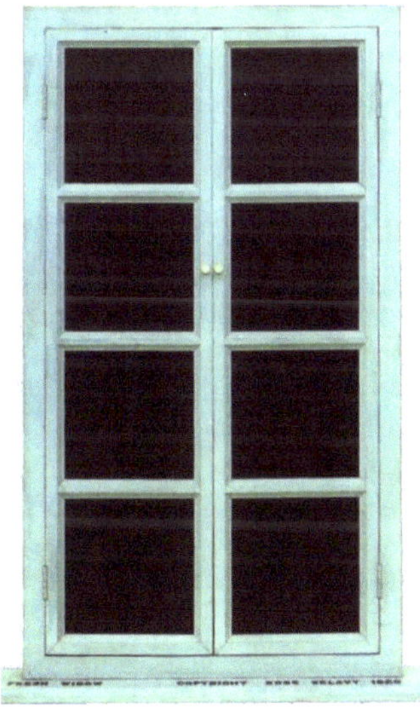

Fresh Widow presents a small French window whose glass panes have been replaced with panels of opaque black leather. The work was made shortly after Duchamp returned to New York and was labeled on the base "COPYRIGHT ROSE SELAVY 1920." The substitution of leather for glass turns a domestic object associated with light and openness into one of obstruction and withdrawal.

The title and the darkened windows suggest mourning, an undertone first seen in *Morée*'s black border. What began there as a quiet signal of loss becomes here a literal closure: windows that cannot open, panes that cannot reveal. The covering is physical, not pictorial; the act of concealment has become the work itself.

Marcel Duchamp & Man Ray, The Gift (1921)

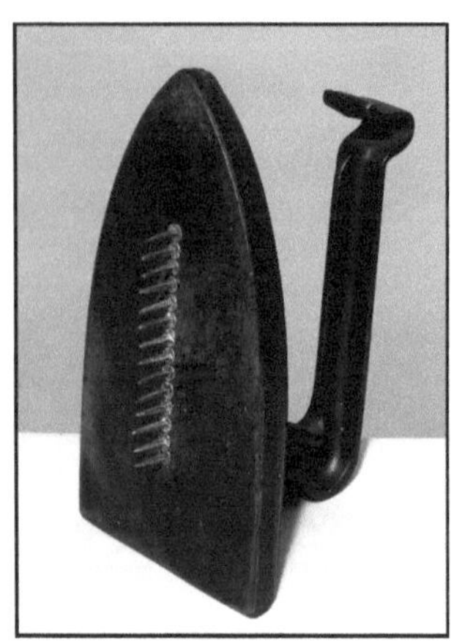

The flat iron fitted with a line of tacks transforms a useful household object into one that can no longer perform its purpose. The alteration neutralizes its everyday role, converting an instrument of care into one of harm.

This deliberate obstruction exemplifies **Denial of Function**—a precise, almost surgical gesture that renders the familiar inoperative.

In *Morée*, the same logic unfolds at the level of image and authorship. The painting's surface, once capable of serving as a decorative or expressive object, is deliberately compromised: its signature scraped, its elegance unsettled by drips and abrasion. What might have been a viable image of refinement is recast as a site of refusal.

Both works hinge on a minimal act that converts completion into negation. In *The Gift*, utility is undone; in *Morée*, decorum is dismantled. Each turns the act of making into an act of withholding—an assertion that art, like function, can be deliberately broken.

Man Ray, Pearl Necklace, (1924)
published in Picabia's 391

A nearly full-page
photograph of a pearl
necklace appeared in *391*,
signed "Man Ray, Paris." It
is presented without
commentary or surrounding
text, functioning almost as a
stand-alone graphic. The
image may echo *Morée*
through its focus on the same
motif—the suspended string
of pearls—now reduced to a
direct photographic

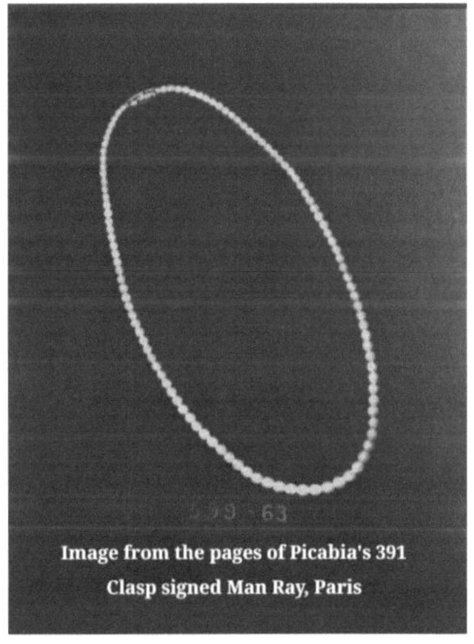

Image from the pages of Picabia's 391
Clasp signed Man Ray, Paris

statement. Whether or not it was intentional, the
repetition suggests that the visual language first tested
in *Morée* remained active within the circle years later.

The Disguise Perfected:
Étant donnés

Decades later, Duchamp completes the long retreat that began with *Morée* in his final work, *Étant donnés: 1° la chute d'eau / 2° le gaz d'éclairage…*

Here, illusion has become structure. Visitors approach a heavy wooden door, sealed except for two small holes. Through them, they glimpse a nude figure illuminated in a constructed landscape — visible, yet unreachable. What was once painted on a surface has become an environment, a scene that can only be viewed through restriction.

Every part of the installation enforces distance. The viewer's position is fixed, their sight controlled by the apparatus itself. The peepholes dictate not only what can be seen but how it must be seen — a choreography of perception reduced to a single axis of vision.

By limiting the viewer's point of view, Duchamp exposes the limits of painting itself: the illusion of depth sustained only through restriction. The three-dimensional scene thus becomes a literalized painting — a spatial trap that turns freedom of sight into obedience.

In *Étant donnés,* vision is no longer passive but captive. The act of looking is bound to a single aperture, where revelation and confinement become one and the same.

Closing The Circle

By converting illusion into physical construction, Duchamp completes a circuit that began decades earlier.

- To the casual viewer, *Étant donnés* is a voyeuristic scene built for shock and mystery.

- To those who know *Morée*, it reads as deliberate closure — the turning of an idea into a secret.

The work functions as both culmination and concealment. The strategies that first appeared in *Morée* — distance, obstruction, and the refusal of easy vision — return here as final form. What began as a theatrical illusion ends as a physical barrier. The system is complete, and the secret, once staged in paint, is now locked in space.

Yet this closure also redefines authorship. By fixing the viewer's position and sealing the scene, Duchamp transforms the artist from maker into architect of perception. The work no longer represents — it conditions experience. What had once been an image is now a device: an engine that controls time, space, and desire.

The disguise, perfected, becomes indistinguishable from revelation. In the end, *Étant donnés* is not a tableau but a mechanism — one that ensures the act of looking will always remain incomplete.

Dating and Verification

The convergence of *Mistinguett* and *Theorem* fixes *Morée's* probable creation between mid-1915 and late-1916, during Duchamp's New York residence. Both works echo *Morée's* ideas and techniques, implying it circulated within the Arensberg circle before 1917. Formally and conceptually, *Morée* also sits between Nude Descending a Staircase, No. 2 (1912) and No. 3 (1916). If Duchamp is the artist, the punctuation ("..Morée…") situates the work between the two Nudes.

A Favor, Ruhl & Co. artboard stamp on the reverse matches the earlier of two known variants, used roughly 1914–1922. Comparable examples appear on a separate group of Favor, Ruhl boards—Ziegfeld Follies costume designs naming performers active in those years—and on one unrelated but dated example from 1922, placing *Morée's* support firmly within that range.

Scientific examination has not yet been conducted. No pigment or binder testing, ultraviolet imaging, or forensic study of the stamp has been performed. Each could refine the current inference, especially regarding the casein/oil layering and oxidation patterns. Until such testing occurs, the dating remains inferential but strong: *Morée* precedes the 1917 works that quote it and functions as the hinge between Nude No. 2 and Nude No. 3.

Part II
Passage from Virgin To Bride:
From Nude Descending a Staircase to The Large Glass

Following the evidence of *Morée*, this section turns to Duchamp's own sequence of transformations—from *Nude Descending a Staircase* to *The Large Glass.* It proposes a direct continuity between these works, interpreting the shift from the Nude to the Bride as a deliberate transformation rather than a rupture — a reading in which Duchamp appears to absorb the public's misreading and turn it into structure.

When *Nude Descending a Staircase, No. 2* was rejected from the 1912 Salon des Indépendants and later mocked in New York as a "machine gone mad," Duchamp paid close attention. The public had mistaken his experiment in time and movement for a depiction of machinery. Rather than correct them, he seems to have absorbed the misreading.

In this reading, the figure once called mechanical now becomes mechanical by design. In *The Passage from Virgin to Bride* (1912), Duchamp translates motion into metamorphosis: the momentum of descent becomes suspension, the body converting from organic to mechanical form.

In *The Bride* (1912, Philadelphia Museum of Art), this transformation becomes overt. The figure once animated by descent now stands suspended in a state of conversion — her contours replaced by articulated planes and armature-like structures. The supple rhythms of the *Nude* yield to an architecture of precision: measured divisions, mechanical symmetry, a body reimagined as instrument. Duchamp seems to give the audience what they thought they saw — a woman turned machine, but by intention rather than accident.

The irony is unmistakable. What critics mistook in *Nude Descending a Staircase* becomes the premise of the next work. Misreading is absorbed as method; the error becomes productive. The *Nude* was called mechanical, so Duchamp constructed a *Bride* who is mechanical by design.

Here, movement turns inward. Instead of traversing space, it circulates through an enclosed system of joints and couplings — a choreography of controlled resistance. This internalization of motion anticipates *The Large Glass*, where the Bride and the Bachelors become separate but synchronized mechanisms: the visible architecture of desire and its delay.

Bride Stripped Bare by Her Bachelors, Even
(The Large Glass)

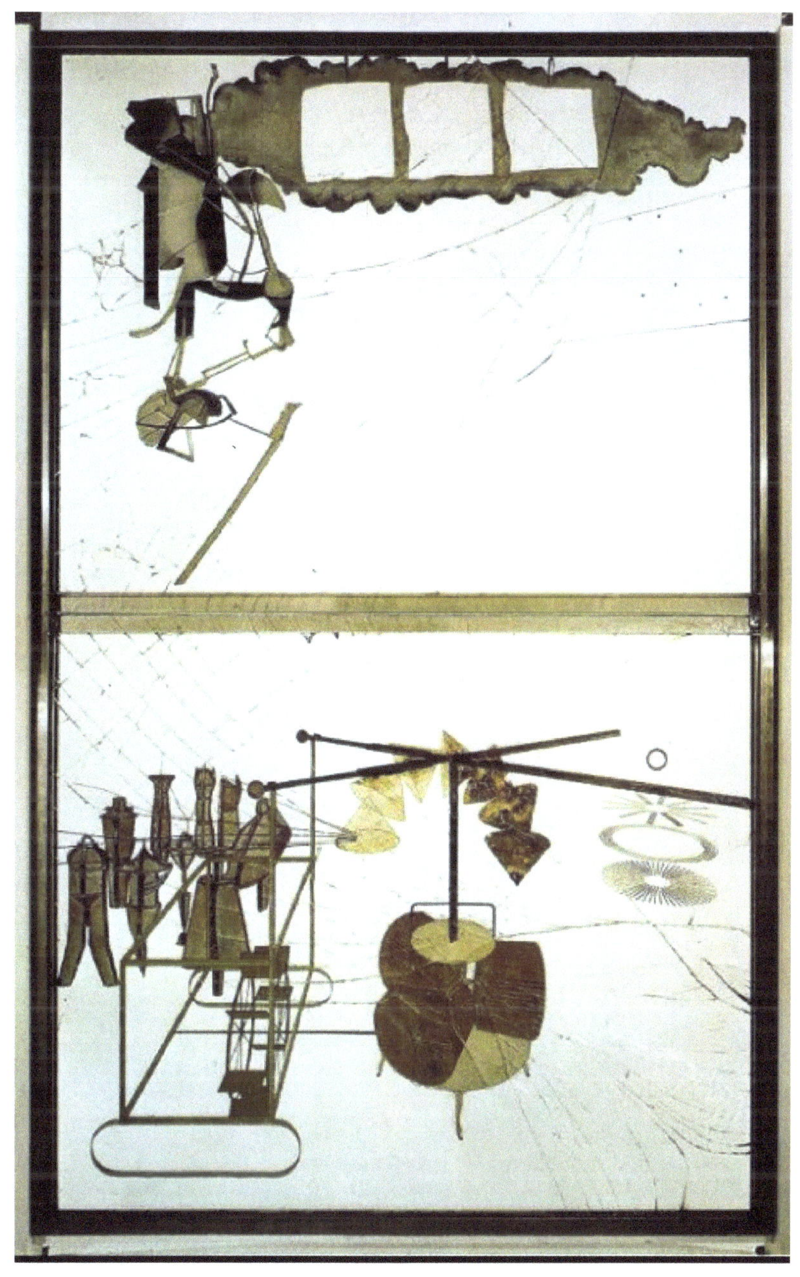

Marcel Duchamp — Philadelphia Museum of Art, Philadelphia, PA

Toward *The Large Glass*:
The Public as Bachelors

With *The Bride* (1912), Duchamp accepts and redirects the public's earlier misreading. The mechanical idiom once projected onto his work becomes his deliberate grammar. In *The Bride*, human presence gives way to a structural order — a schematic articulation of parts, calibrated rather than expressive.

In *The Large Glass (The Bride Stripped Bare by Her Bachelors, Even)* (1915–23), this logic expands into full system. The upper register holds the Bride, suspended and inaccessible; below her stand the Bachelors, mechanical surrogates of desire, endlessly engaged in futile operation. The transparent plane preserves their mutual visibility yet enforces separation.

The Bachelors can be read as the public itself — looking, desiring, misinterpreting, and thereby animating the work. The Bride, remote and autonomous, becomes the artwork as object of projection. What once appeared accidental now reveals its structure: a machine designed to expose the gap between seeing and knowing. *The Large Glass* completes the shift from depiction to mechanism, making misunderstanding the engine of modern perception.

Delay as Structure

Duchamp described The Large Glass as a "delay in glass." The phrase defines the logic of the work: a system designed to hold energy in suspension. Nothing in the composition resolves. The Bachelors below are locked in repetitive motion; the Bride above remains unreachable. Every mechanism functions, but nothing happens.

This deliberate non-event marks Duchamp's full departure from representation. The work does not depict a scene — it constructs a process. Desire, miscommunication, and failure are not themes but operating principles. The transparent surface makes this system literal: the painting is no longer a window but a barrier, exposing the mechanics of looking while denying completion.

In this form, Duchamp converts painting into a controlled experiment. The image has become a structure; motion has become procedure. The Large Glass concludes the transformation that began with the Nude — a shift from depicting movement to organizing meaning through delay.

Summary:
From Motion to System

Across the decade from 1912 to 1923, Duchamp moves from representing movement to constructing systems that suspend it. Nude Descending a Staircase translates motion into visual rhythm; The Bride mechanizes that rhythm into abstract form; and The Large Glass turns the entire process into a controlled structure of deferral.

What begins as an exploration of physical descent becomes a study of intellectual distance. Duchamp's withdrawal from painting parallels the Bride's separation from the Bachelors: both enact a calculated delay between cause and effect, image and interpretation.

By leaving *The Large Glass* "definitively unfinished," Duchamp extended this suspension into time itself—transforming incompletion into a system. The work's very incompletion becomes its engine: a perpetual deferral of closure that mirrors the separation of the Bride and the Bachelors. What began as motion in *Nude Descending a Staircase* ends as conceptual stillness, a closed circuit of desire without resolution.

A Note on Picabia's *Mistinguett*

The dating of Francis Picabia's *Mistinguett* has remained uncertain for decades. The painted inscription "Francis Picabia 1917," though authentic in hand, appears to have been applied over an already aged surface — the paint sinking into existing cracks rather than lying atop fresh layers. This anomaly, combined with the portrait's stylistic proximity to Picabia's pre-Dada period, has led many scholars to reject the 1917 date and instead place the work around 1908–1911.

Viewed in relation to *Morée*, however, the evidence points to a different resolution. *Mistinguett* likely originated as an earlier conventional portrait that Picabia revisited and transformed in 1917. The dense black pool, the scraped and fingerprinted passages, and the network of vertical drips all appear to have been added at that time — interventions too radical to belong to his earlier manner, yet perfectly aligned with the acts of removal, abrasion, and coded defacement first seen in *Morée*.

Under this reading, the 1917 inscription is not a false date but a record of reactivation — the moment Picabia converted a pre-war image into a Dada surface. The year ceases to be an enigma and becomes a point at which *Morée*'s private language was documented for posterity.

Note on Sources

All works discussed in this study are publicly documented and accessible. The argument is drawn entirely from established visual and historical evidence already in the public domain. No claims rely on unpublished archives, private correspondence, or material unavailable for independent verification.

The purpose of this booklet is not to reveal hidden documents but to reconsider what is already visible — to look again at familiar works whose relationships have gone unrecognized.

Nude Descending a Staircase No. 2
Marcel Duchamp — Philadelphia Museum of Art, Philadelphia, PA

Morée
Marcel Duchamp — Privately Owned

Nude Descending a Staircase No. 3
Marcel Duchamp — Philadelphia Museum of Art, Philadelphia, PA

Theorem
Walter Arensberg, 1917 issue No. 2 of Blind Man

Mistinguett
Francis Picabia — Solomon R. Guggenheim Museum, New York, NY

Da-Dandy
Hannah Hoch — Privately Owned

Belle Haleine
Man Ray, Marcel Duchamp — Museum of Modern Art, New York, NY

Fresh Widow
Marcel Duchamp — Museum of Modern Art, New York, NY

Cadeau (Gift)
Man Ray — Original Lost

Pearl Necklace Photograph
Man Ray, 1924 issue No. 19 of Picabia's 391 (last issue)

Bride Stripped Bare by Her Bachelors, Even
Marcel Duchamp — Philadelphia Museum of Art, Philadelphia, PA

www.ingramcontent.com/pod-product-compliance
Lightning Source LLC
Chambersburg PA
CBHW040916110726
48005CB00006B/910